LOVE & LIFE THRU THE EYEZ OF LYRIK

A COLLECTION OF POETRY, ENCOURAGING REMINDERS, AND LIFE JOURNEY NOTES

VOLUME 1

Krystal "Lyrik Hunter" Dorsey

LOVE & LIFE THRU THE EYEZ OF LYRIK

Pieces from my Healing Journey 2015-2022

©2022 Krystal "LyriK Hunter" Dorsey

All rights reserved. No part of this book may be reproduced or transmitted in any form or by any means, graphic, electronic, or mechanical, including photocopying, recording, taping or by any information storage retrieval system, without express permission from the publisher except for brief quotations that are embodied in critical articles and reviews.

For information about permission to reproduce selections from this book or purchase for education use, please email:
thebrownsugahlounge@gmail.com

First Paperback edition November 2022
ISBN: 979-8-9851987-7-5

Written/Edited by: Krystal "Lyrik Hunter" Dorsey
Photography: Reign Ifa, Erica Johnson, Knotted Tree Studios
Cover Design: Shuga Shuga Publishing

Published by Shuga Shuga Publishing LLC
ssbookpllc@gmail.com
web: shugashugallc.com
phone: (214)727-4496

Table of Contents

Introduction/Backstory i
LOVE & LIFE THRU THE EYEZ OF LYRIK v

PART 1 "LIFE"

🖤 LIFE 🖤 1
🖤 FRAGILE HEART-DEPRESSION 🖤 3
🖤 FADING TO DARKNESS/THE RAIN IS GONE 🖤 5
🖤 I BEEN THINKING 🖤 7
🖤 NOBODY EVA TOLD ME 🖤 9
🖤NOTE TO SELF🖤 11

PART 2 "PAIN"

🖤PAIN🖤 13
🖤NOTE TO SELF🖤 14
🖤U GOT ME FUCKED UP🖤 16
🖤UNHEALED WOUNDS🖤 18
🖤WE NEED A FIX🖤 19
🖤 MESSAGE TO A NARCISSIST 🖤 20
🖤 DEAR PAIN 🖤 22
🖤TAKING OUT THE TRASH🖤 24
🖤 TIMING 🖤 25
🖤 SHOTS FIRED 🖤 26

PART 3 "FREE YOUR MIND"

♥ FREE YOUR MIND ♥ 30
♥ SELF REFLECTION ♥ 32

PART 4 LOVE (PEACE AND LIGHT)

♥ LOVE ♥ 35
♥ A SISTER'S LOVE ♥ 36
♥ TELL ME IT'S REAL ♥ 40
♥ WINDOWS, GLASS, & SUNSHINE ♥ 41
♥ PEACE ♥ 42
♥ RECOVERY ♥ 43
♥ I LIED ♥ 44
♥ LIGHT ♥ 45
♥ BINGO ♥ 46
♥ AFTER THE STORM ♥ 48
♥ TRY AGAIN ♥ 50
♥ FOCUS ♥ 52
♥ PROMISES I'M GLAD I MADE TO MYSELF ♥ 53

Dedications & Appreciations 56
ABOUT THE AUTHOR 58
SPONSORSHIP/DONATION ACKNOWLEDGEMENTS 59
PERSONAL SPONSORS 63
LAUNCH TEAM 64

Introduction/Backstory

It was 2005, three years after my husband and I had split, two young boys at that time and my life was spiraling out of control (so I thought). I was faced with making some very personal decisions regarding life and I was not fit to manage it emotionally or financially.

For the first time ever, I was dealing with depression, constantly making poor decisions, stifling my personal growth, and allowing others to keep me in that space because I couldn't save myself. It felt like I was digging a grave and allowing the people around me to pile the dirt on top, burying me alive. I was dying inside and no one around me knew it. I was certain that I wouldn't make it out alive. So, when two children turned into three and I found myself back inside that hole, I was ready to let it all go. I wrote letters to my children in the event that one day they woke up and I was gone. I cried as I wrote those letters to them in my journal and the tears continued to fall for days. The days turned into weeks and then to months and they continued for years after.

By 2008, It was apparent that I had some things I needed to deal with inside of me that was gonna take more than a blunt and a glass of fireball to cure. But like most everyone else in the Black community, seeing a therapist was not an option ... so I sucked it up. I told myself, "you'll be fine girl, it's all good." I thought if I told myself that long enough, that what I was facing would magically disappear, just like everything and everyone else in my life that I tried so hard to hold onto that wasn't good to me or for me.

That was just the beginning!!

By 2010, I had been through five additional failed relationships and for the life of me, I just couldn't understand what it was that I was doing wrong!!

The year 2015 crept up on me like a thief in the night. I had gone through two more failed relationships and a current partner who was putting me through my third year of hell on earth with him, and all I was doing was

continuing to let him do it. I couldn't quite put my finger on why I was allowing this man to put me back into that grave I dug for myself years ago. I wasn't sure if I could pull myself out this time. It was deep. This man was a master manipulator, and he knew all the right things to say to cover up all the wrong shit he was doing to me. Even when he didn't have anything to say, he found ways to keep me tangled up in his web of lies and deceit. There's some truth in the saying, "people will treat you exactly how you let them", and I allowed it. I allowed and accepted every single bit of it.

One day, a good friend of mine that I hadn't spoken to in months, called to check on me. I'll never forget that day. I answered the phone with a fake smile on my face, pretending to be okay, inside I was hoping he would come and take this pain away. His next words were, "ARE YOU OKAY?" ... Fighting back tears, I replied, "Yea, I'm good, how are you?" He followed with, "ARE YOU ABLE TO SPEAK FREELY," and I replied, "NO." He knew something was wrong, I'm sure he could hear it in my trembling voice, so he advised me to take a ride to the store and call him when I was in a safe space to speak.

For the first time in a long time, I FELT SEEN WITHOUT EVEN BEING PHYSICALLY SEEN. He convinced me somehow that I was not okay and that I deserved better than what I was accepting, better than what I was allowing, and it was time for me to save myself. I knew I deserved better, but something inside of me had me feeling like what I had was all I was worthy of having. I felt like I was supposed to go through all this shit, ride it out and one day, I'd end up on the other side of the rainbow, holding my pot of Gold!

Many others had told me before then to let that man go and I would not listen. That day it was different. I was at my breaking point and if I didn't make some decisions quick, there wasn't gonna be a happy ending for me.

I drove back home after that conversation not really knowing what I was going to do. I put up with that man and all his toxic ass behavior for a few more traumatizing months. Soon after, I had to take a trip back to my hometown after news that my uncle passed. While I was away from home, dealing with the death of my uncle, he was back in Dallas doing his thing as usual. I was trying to cope with grieving the loss of my loved one and grieving over a relationship that was doomed from the start. My heart was breaking with every tear that fell from my eyes!

I played "WHAT IS LOVE" by V. Bozeman on repeat for two hours, maybe even longer, each time singing it louder, singing it stronger. I was singing through my tears at the top of my lungs. I cried so much that day that it felt like I had no tears left to cry. My body was weak, brittle, and breaking. I couldn't function long enough to have a normal conversation.

When it was time to make that 5-hour drive back to Dallas, I only had one thing on my mind and that was to get my life in order.

To do that I had to shed some dead skin and let go of the weight that was weighing me down. This meant unpacking all those bags I had been carrying around for the past 10 years prior and wash all that dirty laundry. Start fresh and it was imperative that I started with the most important piece of my life. ME!! Because you see, without me, the people around me that mattered the most, couldn't be cared for or loved properly, because it ALL started with me.

My cup was empty, and there was nothing there to pour into others because my soul was not being replenished. All I ever wanted was for someone to LOVE ME. But how could I expect anyone to love me, if I didn't even love myself.

I HAD TO START WITH ME
THAT IS WHERE MY JOURNEY TO HEALING BEGAN
IT STARTED WITH ME

I'm giving you pieces of me that I've not shared with many... that's probably why it took me so long to finally put this book together. But we're here now, so let's dive in... THIS IS WHAT HEALING LOOKS LIKE TO ME AND THE JOURNEY STILL CONTINUES TODAY.

Let's take a stroll...

MAY THIS BOOK BE HEALING FOR YOUR MIND, BODY, AND SOUL

By the way, I'm Lyrik ... COME TAKE A WALK WITH ME!

LOVE & LIFE THRU THE EYEZ OF LYRIK
VOLUME 1

#LETSHEAL

Dear Me (Past, Present, and Future)!

How beautiful it is to watch you grow year after year. You're doing such an excellent job coping with life and finding creative ways to maintain a positive and healthy space for us to live in. You are nourishing Your mind, body, and soul in ways that we never imagined possible. Just a few years ago, I remember when we thought we'd never make it out of that dark place alive, now look at us!! Out here living our best lives, conquering fears, marking things off the bucket list, traveling the world, excelling in the corporate world, crushing these entrepreneurial goals, and making a new list of things to accomplish every single day.

I just want you to know how proud I am!! You never gave up on us, you found a way to keep fighting when you wanted to give up and it's because of you that we are still here! If you had given up, we would have never seen all the things and experienced the colors of this life and all its beauty that exists outside the walls that held us captive for way too long. You are a warrior, you are resilient, and you are strong!! There is no darkness on this earth that can stop you from shining.

Today, it's time to give yourself the love you deserve, the recognition you have earned, the appreciation you are owed! You have spent most of your life supporting, uplifting, and encouraging everyone else and now it's finally your turn! Give yourself some love, and lots of it, just like you do for everyone else. Self-Love and Humility have signed a new lease, and from

this day forward they will reside together, in the same space and you will be covered in greatness from head to toe.

Stand up straight.
Look yourself in the mirror.
Let us see that great big, beautiful smile.
Now take what's rightfully yours.

YOU ARE EVERYTHING WE DREAMED YOU COULD BE AND YOU HAVEN'T EVEN REACHED YOUR PEAK YET. HANG ON TIGHT AND BUCKLE UP FOR THE RIDE. WE JUST GETTING STARTED SO #LETSRIDE!

KEEP SHINING! THIS IS FOR YOU! CONGRATULATIONS GODDESS! NOW PAT YOURSELF ON THE BACK AND GET READY FOR THE NEXT LEVEL! #LETSGLOWUP #KEEPSHINING

I LOVE YOU!

Sincerely,
Me

PART 1

"LIFE"

 LIFE

When you have allowed things to congest your mind to the point where your vision is clouded, it leaves no space for reality to exist. You are soon covered in total darkness; nothing but negative thoughts and doubt takes over all the positive, healthy, and beautiful places your soul used to reside. You have evicted life from your body so many times that you begin to believe that this is the way you are supposed to be living. "NO VACANCIES", is what the sign plastered to the outside of the walls said hanging on my heart. These walls have been under permanent construction for so many years because I refused to trust anyone enough to help me repair the multi-layered damages created over the years.

One day, I chose me over everyone else and firmly said to my inner child, "STOP....NO MORE...IT'S TIME TO LET GO AND LIVE... NOT FOR ANYONE ELSE...FOR YOURSELF!!!"

If this is you, it's time to Put yourself at the top of the priority list and let all the negative thoughts and darkness go.

LOVE YOURSELF....LIVE YOUR LIFE

EVERYONE WILL NOT AGREE WITH YOUR CHOICES, BUT THEY WILL HAVE NO CHOICE BUT TO RESPECT IT... PREPARE YOURSELF FOR THE GROWTH THAT IS AWAITING YOU ON THE ROAD TO YOUR DESTINY AND LET THE RECOVERY BEGIN TODAY

IT'S TIME!

JOURNEY NOTE:

Life .... a journey unknown .... a never-ending road .....an experience which we often wonder about. Sometimes day-dreaming about....

Life ... It teaches us our weaknesses and our strengths ... it provides understanding when we may have given up on ever finding a way to understand.

When there is darkness all around us, oftentimes if we just keep going and feed our minds well, life finds a creative way to bring light to our path. KEEP GOING...LIFE TEACHES US OUR BEST LESSONS, WHEN WE JUST GO THROUGH IT AND GROW THROUGH IT!! U GOT THIS!

♥ FRAGILE HEART-DEPRESSION ♥

When the lights go out and nothing but darkness fills the empty space between your eyes and your imagination....it seems as if I've been here before, but nothing in my soul can replace the feeling I had before I made it to this point. I tried to forget about those memories that haunted me every second of the day...everything that reminded me of how my highest point of happiness somehow turned into my lowest point of sadness. How did I allow someone to lead me down this path of depression all over again, when I promised myself, I would never let myself down like that ever again.

Still, I fell.

I fell down and I stayed there, until I could no longer feel my fingers, hands, or legs.

I laid there until my entire body was numb.... I couldn't feel a thing... NO HEARTBEAT, NO BLOOD PUMPING THROUGH MY VEINS, NO POWER FIGHTING TO GET OUT OF MY SPIRIT, NO STRENGTH...... NO ANGER, NO LAUGHTER, NO HAPPINESS... NOT A PIECE OF FEELING LEFT or any other emotion that makes LOVE or HAPPINESS WORTH HAVING IN THIS LIFE.

How did I get here and how do I get back to my sunshine? It was the only thing that gave me some hope at really seeing the things in front of me.... VISION, CLARITY...I NEED TO SEE WHAT I USED TO SEE INSIDE OF ME... I know it's hiding somewhere in there, down deep ...But I can't find the strength to dig down deep enough to pull it back out. I can't find the strength to get back to me. I'm staring myself in the mirror and I still can't see!!

FRAGILE
HANDLE WITH CARE

LOVE & LIFE THRU THE EYEZ OF LYRIK

♥ FADING TO DARKNESS/THE RAIN IS GONE

Behind my eyelids, closed, shut so tight, attempting to suffocate the tears that are forcefully trying to burst through, and I keep telling myself that I can win this fight. Convincing myself is the hardest part because even though I still feel the beat of my heart pounding through my chest it's so hollow inside those walls, and then I felt the rain drops fall. In a feeling of defeat, a million teardrops begin to crawl, flooding my face and landing on the pillowcase that I have buried myself deep inside ... it now resembles a deep grave, a hole so deep that it's like a groundhog's hiding place.

It's SOOO deep...so deep that it's beginning to consume every ounce of joy that I have left inside of me... I am fighting to regain the pieces of the puzzle that make up the beautiful picture, but they are scattered, misplaced, and hidden from my reach...and I'm thinking to myself this has to be a breach ... A breach of the contract that was signed when I burst into adulthood and took an oath to live and be responsible and accountable for my actions, children, and home...

I was so certain that I could take on all the curve balls thrown my way and all the challenges that might occur from day to day, but that was before, and I was fine until Today... Today, all I want to do is curl up in a ball and CRY...SCREAM OUT WHY ME, WHY DOES IT HAVE TO BE THIS WAY? I'm afraid to let the light shine in because even with one happy moment comes the fear multiplied by ten. I lay in my bed standing clear of the outsiders, refusing to allow anyone to get too close...unsure of who to trust because even the ones I've loved have hurt me the most.

AND THEN, I HEAR MUSIC playing very faintly in the background...and I'm thankful for the sound that it gives because it's the only thing keeping me from breaking down. The music...I can hear it and it's the only thing that

keeps me moving... I'M trying to get closer to it...moving slowly, as the sound begins to get louder. ... (WITH A SIGH OF RELIEF) I can feel it and it's soothing .. I can feel the freedom as the tears begin to slowly come to a halt...eyes still shut tight, but with just a little push, I might be able to open them up before I fall. One blink, two blinks, three blinks, four...now the music's loud and clear and my soul wants to hear more... And before I hit the floor... The speakers blast louder than before and the words that I hear, save my life, as I shed the last tear, I can finally see the light

(SINGING) I CAN SEE CLEARLY NOW THE RAIN IS GONE... :-

 I BEEN THINKING

I been thinking about taking a walk today ... a slow and steady walk down memory lane ... but today just ain't the day .. can't seem to get through the walk without breaking down, so I think for now it's best that I stay in my own lane, so I don't have to try and decipher the happiness from the pain...

But I been thinking
I been thinking today I'll sit with my own thoughts and my journal and write down all the things that come to mind.... Good, bad, and in between, and maybe eventually, one day I'll get it all out of my head, so I can at least get a good night's rest tonight when I go to bed ... But writing down pages full of pain don't always come out easy, so I've decided I'd rather take a break for today.

But I been thinking
I been thinking that maybe just one day, I'll build up enough courage to face my fears, believe in myself, appreciate who I am, love myself a little more, do something sweet, just for me, instead of trying to make everyone else happy around me. I tried it before, but things didn't go as planned, BUT this time, I'm going to try harder, be consistent, and stay focused on being better today.

I BEEN THINKIN' ....
I've been thinkin today is the best day to be amazing, sing my heart out, write until my fingers cramp up, revisit all those moments that made me who I am, because I'm worth it ... Because knowing your own secrets and facing your own demons, is what creates greatness when no one else is watching .... Never thought I'd ever see that bright night star closeup. She's more beautiful than I ever imagined ... Like a Lavender, concrete Rose ..

Today, I think it's time to bloom ... grow towards the sun. Maybe it's time I rise, squeeze through the tight spaces and cracks in the universe, changing space and time, maybe it's my time.

BECAUSE I BEEN THINKIN'
Today may be the perfect day to pack up all that pain and put it somewhere safe. Put all my happiness on the fireplace mantel, get cozy, burn away my fears, and make room for my never-ending light to shine

Today, it's time that I finally listen, I think that I've actually done more than enough thinkin'

🖤 NOBODY EVA TOLD ME 🖤

Nobody eva told me about the pain this fucked up world would place on me. Neva told me mastering survival wasn't even half of the life lessons and hacks that I needed to keep my heart in one piece. They neva taught me how to fully love myself. I've spent years afraid that the people I loved the most would one day choose to leave me just like my daddy did

Childhood memories took up space in my cluttered brain reminding me of how my daddy issues kept on keeping me in my own way ... robbing me of the beauty of a healthy relationship in so many ways ... And I was too busy trying to prove my obvious worth, spent way too much time begging unworthy folks to stay

They neva told me ...
Neva told me about how I would somehow, in my darkest moments, find reasons to question my judgment when I knew damn well that none of them ever loved me... I had all that dirty laundry piled up and didn't even wanna wash it ... I'd rather just go shopping, it felt better to buy a new outfit, at least that way I felt cleaned up and fresh to death, no matter what my life looked like outside those threads ... man,

I just wish they woulda told me

Maybe it woulda kept me from feeling like they neva loved me and today I'd have a beautiful life with somebody, instead of constantly feeling like I might die lonely. I beat myself up too long for not understanding the things that nobody eva told me .... Wish I'd learned those lessons sooner instead of suffering all those years and trying to shake that shit (depression) up off me

So today, I'm saying FUCK IT ... I'd rather just lay here and let you hold me ...I'll figure the rest of that shit out when I wake up in the morning!

♥NOTE TO SELF♥

(All Cried Out)

After all the tears have dried and there's nothing left but the stains on the pillowcases left behind and the silence in between the walls that you have closed yourself inside.....you eventually have to find the strength to get up and MOVE ON. Even though your mind and the brokenness of your mishandled heart continues to make you believe that you just can't move on.... Don't believe it!! YOU DESERVE TO GLIDE INTO THE SPACES OF YOUR OWN GREATNESS....THE SPACES WHERE ALL YOUR BLESSINGS RESIDE... BUT, before you can successfully take the first step toward moving on, you must do the unthinkable.... the one thing that you have continued to believe you could never do no matter how small or big it seemed. YOU SIMPLY HAVE TO PUSH ALL OF THE NEGATIVITY ASIDE AND CHOOSE TO FORGIVE!!

FORGIVE WITHOUT EXPECTING AN APOLOGY. FORGIVE WITHOUT EXPECTING A CHANGE IN BEHAVIOR. FORGIVE EVEN IF IT HURTS TO THINK ABOUT IT AND DO IT FOR YOUR OWN PERSONAL GROWTH.

WITHOUT FORGIVENESS, YOU ARE STRANDED IN A SEA OF QUICKSAND, WAITING TO DROWN IN YOUR OWN BITTERNESS AND SORROW.

GRASP YOUR FUTURE... FORGIVE FREELY AND LIVE!!!!

PART 2

"PAIN"

 PAIN

Pain can make you feel like life is caving in all around you, crushing the walls around your heart, and burying you alive as you try to keep breathing. Sometimes you have to die to feel alive again. Sometimes you have to feel all the pain to restore your soul.... feel it all. The journey will not always be easy ... be willing to lose it all in order to win. More often than not, your life depends on it, you just have to be strong enough to GET THROUGH IT!! DON'T GIVE UP!

(Questions during the painful stage)

If I peeled away the layers of my smooth caramel skin, would you be willing to see what lies underneath? Would you attempt to understand what's hiding within? Would the invisible scars from the pain that I've endured, leave you in a state of disbelief and misunderstandings? Would you be capable of being the strength that I need when all the others chose to abuse or misuse me? Are you able to make loving me a priority? What would you do?

♥NOTE TO SELF♥

(Preparing to Heal)

Seems like I had found a way to hide all of my pain, tears, and heartache by masking it; burying it behind the shadow of my busy work & home schedule & spending any of the free time I had sleeping & partying as much as I could. Not saying that I don't deserve to hang out and have fun because if anyone knows me u know I'm determined to enjoy my life to the fullest but this time, avoiding the fact that I was hurting was the one thing that I was making a point to do. So here I am, finally getting back to me and learning to rediscover the "ME" that I had found & lost again a couple of years ago, and yes it can be difficult. It's like waking up each morning, getting dressed, and then walking out the house only to realize once u get to work that u left your favorite pair of earrings on the restroom countertop. Like DAAAAAAMMMNNNN what is going on? I'm missing something here!!

Long story short, I'm taking a personal vow to never allow myself to even get close to losing myself again. I will do everything in my power to keep my self-love at an all-time high, and I will always consult God/Universe and listen to my intuition in every decision that I make along the way. I will admit, I lost myself somewhere along the way and I'm not ashamed, but I will never ever misplace her or let her run away from me again.

♥U GOT ME FUCKED UP♥

When your mind won't allow you to overlook even the smallest shit, because you're so used to being fucked over that everything that's really "nothing" turns into something. When you find yourself tiptoeing around certain conversations that need to be had, too afraid of what might come out of your mouth, mental capacity so fragile that you don't have the strength to just let shit be what it's gonna be. When your heart wants to flutter at the sweetest gestures of romance, instead you're too busy trying to analyze why they did what they did to begin with, assuming they are trying to do something nice to cover up some fucked-up shit they did to you the night before.

Why else would they just stop by to say hello out the blue? Because they're just thinking of you? Or why would they even bother sending you flowers to your job? Just to show how much they care? And why the hell would they have your bath water ran and waiting on you with your favorite type of wine if they didn't do nothing wrong? That's what's going on in my mind at the time. So, I take a moment, try to breathe, think about how I'm acting before I act a damn fool. I say, "thank you" and "oh that was so sweet of you", or "that was very thoughtful of you to do that". I say, "oh you didn't have to do that", and I ignore that other side of me that wants to start asking a million questions and waiting for him to mess up, because nigga you just can't be that nice for no reason at all.

I ain't dumb! U got me fucked all the way up...

Yeah, I pushed that shit to the side, I believed he gave a damn, and now fast forward look where the hell I am. Sitting here pouring out my soul, heart, and tears onto this paper because just like I thought, that dude was full of games, bullshit, and whole lot of damn spam.... That muthafucka

bamboozled me! Nothing he ever said to me was true .... he was on some more shit and yeah I shoulda knew. I shoulda kept that wall up like I started to do, asked all those questions instead of playing it cool.

FOOL ME ONCE SHAME ON YOU, FOOL ME TWICE WELL SHAME ON ME.

BUT FOOL ME 3 TIMES AND I'M COMING FOR YOU....

YOU TOOK SOMETHING FROM ME AND NOW I WANT THAT SHIT BACK.

PREPARE YOURSELF FOR THE WORST, CAUSE NOW THE JOKES ON YOU.

I AIN'T TAKING NO PRISONERS AND I AIN'T TELLING NO LIES...KARMA WILL HAVE IT'S WAY WITH YOU AND THIS TIME, MY EYES ARE ALL OUTTA TEARS TO CRY!!!

♡UNHEALED WOUNDS♡

Wonder if you ever realized how all the mess you've done affects your ability to grow.... You keep making the same mistakes over and over and expecting everyone you hurt to just forget about it and let it go. Nobody asked you for your abuse, misuse of genuine love, your broken promises, or your lies seems like that's all we ever received wrapped up in your very well-tailored and put together disguise.

Ain't nobody asking for no sympathy or for anyone else to give a damn about the pain you caused.... but you walkin' around this bitch like all of a sudden just because you hurtin' now, the world supposed pause.... naw!! ...rethink your approach, because truth be told, you deserve a lot less than what you actually receiving... and the only thing keeping you safe is the fact that folks don't wanna be like you and be deceiving and shit!

Now I ain't saying you the worst in the world, but who's keeping tally marks, especially when you already hurting while someone continues to lay bricks on your heart. All I'm saying is you got "Improvement Needed" written all over your face ... so I think it's best if you get a head start at working on it and be sure to keep a steady pace. No matter how hard you try to cover it up, you still out here cuttin folks that ain't neva hurt you.

IT'S TIME YOU TAKE SOME TIME TO FOCUS ON YOU, take those old ass bandages off and tend to your wounds.

♥WE NEED A FIX♥

Words were spoken and things were said that neither of us were prepared to hear. We took a chance on love again, but we didn't take time to reprogram and now we're here. Confused and lost without EVEN one clue... you blaming me, and I'm damn sure blaming you...We made some mistakes, mishandled some things, and now we're both in limbo because we've allowed those things to stay etched in our brains. We want to love, but can't seem to let go, allowing negative thoughts to consume our minds, and now we're both assuming we know.

No one wants to listen, but no one wants to be the first to say that if we don't repair how we're handling each other, we'll both be walking away. Walking away from what makes us feel whole, knowing we want this more than anyone knows...Work with me please, fight for me as much as I fight for you ... let's give each other a reason to continue pushing through. I don't want to lose you and I don't want to be a fool; I just want you with no secrets or hidden truths wrapped around you. I'VE given you all I have and even pieces of me I didn't know existed, trying my hardest to show you that MY love is consistently always consistent. I can't turn it on and off again, it just doesn't work that way.

I vote we walk together before we choose to walk away!

♥ MESSAGE TO A NARCISSIST ♥

Dafuq was you thinkin'? Ain't no Kings out here doin' shit like this... Now I shoulda blasted ya ass a long time ago, but I been too busy on my grown woman isshhh.

Take off all ya clothes BITCH!

Let the world see you naked... All yo truths and all those lies, hiding in your closet, covered up with all your bullshit and you so damn complacent. You comfortable in that manipulative-ass behavior, huh? ... leading a double life as you feed the world an image of you that's nowhere close to the truth. You told those lies so long, convinced that you could do no wrong, but now you got ya own self believing your fake world is ALL true ...

AW SHIT ... you lookin' for an escape now huh? .. you can't stand the fact that I saw straight through your slop, way before you had a chance to get my mind all twisted up and confused and now you lookin' at the clock...hmm ... Ya timing was off... you didn't check the temperature or the gauges before you let your true colors shine through. Got you busted all up like a blown head gasket, hell you didn't even realize that whole muthafuckin motor blew.... You let me walk right out that door, too stuck up in your ego and pride to correct yourself ... gotchu lookin real stupid now huh...yea nigga you lost that battle, you ain't win that shiny belt....
NOW THAT'S JUST FUCKIN FANTASTIC ... YOU FULL OF IT
.. And if my Brotha was still walkin this earth, I swear he woulda dug up in YO shit!! And you lucky I'm not a vengeful chic, because my Hittas was ready to kick up in yo shit, but I'm good... You ain't even much worth it, my peace is much more important to me than that petty shit. You lost a good one, and I'm gone 4eva remain thankful for that, Ya dig!! Yea gone and suck it in ... Let that seasoning soak in...Baby I'm just too good for you...

was always too much for you, but you was always too stuck on yoself, trying to play games with my mental health and that just didn't get you nowhere...

But knowing you, you'll neva admit it ... and I ain't sticking around for you to get it. Baby girl don't wanna play no more games with you. I'm packed up and I'm gone before you can even think about it boo. Running away from home ain't neva felt this good...so watch me work as I live happily ever after without you.

PS: FUCK YOU

Respectfully,
I PROMISE .. I AIN'T NEVA COMIN BACK FOR YOU!!!

 DEAR PAIN

Today I give thanks!! Thank you to the pain that has held me hostage from my earliest memories as a child. Most of the pain was disguised as love, that was the only way they could get through to me as they smiled.

I trusted many and many let me down ... taking my innocence from me before I even knew what innocence was .. and when I thought I was safe, the monsters were living under the same roof, sleeping in my bed like bed bugs.

They attacked, made it look like something beautiful .. made it feel like something wonderful ... made me feel like I was special, until one day, I realized, I was just an easy target, a bullseye, a bottle lined up on the fence and I was the last challenge ... They took the shot .. and took away from me what I never knew existed because their pleasure was more important than who I would grow up to be. You see .. they never cared about anyone but themselves ... because that woulda been too much trouble for them to even try to think of someone else ... JUST MUTHAFUCKINME SELFISH!!

So, I write this piece for the young girls and young boys whose innocence was stolen before they even learned how to play with their own toys. To those loved ones, cousins, neighbors, and coaches that found manipulative ways to make us feel comfortable ... To the ones that said they loved us, while they misused, abused, and tore us apart .... Just like paper hearts .... but real hearts can't be taped back together, although many of us have tried and failed. It's time that we start wearing those scars, like purple hearts .. that's what we deserve ... we been through war and still came out wearing all those scars like they were cherished awards ... Guess we're the real heroes in the end, because what could have killed us, made us stronger, made us conquerors, made us open our eyes to new possibilities, made us

Kings and Queens with new crowns on our heads to show the world exactly who we are despite our bruises and broken bones! WE MADE IT!

So Dear Pain ... you almost got the best of me, but I'm still here, shining up my war scars ...as I tuck myself in and wish you a good night, I'd like to thank you for preparing me for the fight of my life.

♥TAKING OUT THE TRASH♥

I NEVER LIED WHEN I TOLD YOU I LOVED YOU... I JUST NEVER KNEW THAT YOU WERE NO GOOD FOR ME UNTIL I WAS SICK & TIRED OF BEING HURT BY U ...

AT THE END OF THE DAY, YOU WENT BAD, YOU WERE NO LONGER DIGESTIBLE .... YOUR EDGES WERE MOLDING AND IT WAS NO LONGER SAFE FOR ME TO KEEP TRYING TO CONSUME YOU. TRASH AND TREASURE CAN'T RESIDE IN THE SAME SPACE WITHOUT SOMETHING LOSING VALUE. THERE WAS NOTHING LEFT TO DO, BESIDES WRAP YOU UP AND GET RID OF EVERY BIT OF YOU AND START THE PROCESS OF HEALING AND REPAIRING THE LEAVES THAT HAD BEGAN TO WITHER ON MY BRANCHES!!!

IT'S TIME TO TAKE OUT THE TRASH!!

When your spirit has been filled with so much pain and lies from the past... sometimes you're just not hungry anymore!! At least not for the same thing as before.

Your appetite NOW longs for nourishment, being fed properly becomes MORE important. I DON'T WANT those things that are no longer good for me. Fill me with honesty, love, happiness, knowledge, strength.

Fill me with all the things good for me, that's all I'm hungry for u see. Promise not to starve me!! #FEEDMEWELL or I will be forced to dispose of you!

 TIMING

… He touched me in ways that only a scholar of love could understand. HE'S INTELLIGENT; I LIKE THAT shit!! And in an instant, it was over before it even got started...#TIMING …

🖤 SHOTS FIRED 🖤

(Singing) Don't beat me like a drum, don't strum my pain with your fingers, don't pluck the strings on my guitar, unless your songs will heal my heart

I tried to keep my mouth shut, be the bigger person, went against what I felt in my gut because I didn't want to be the one looked at as bitter.

God forbid the Black Woman ever being so hurt that it causes a change in her demeanor. We always have to be SO strong, that our ancestors scream with pride when they see us walking in our greatness, in our strength of all nations. For the most part we do deliver, but it's as if we are never allowed to have moments of weakness. Those moments when we feel like we're drowning in our own blood, we can't seem to let go of the things that we worked so hard for, or the things that we sacrificed our very lives for ... when we've been broken and brushed under the rugs that sit at our front doors that read ... WELCOME!!

And I had welcomed them all into my life ... but by night my day was stripped of its light, because the energy that I had invited in, was now on strike ... non-existent, or maybe it never even really existed, it was all fictitious, a fraud, a lie ... like a fucking reality TV show that's been scripted.

It struck me to my knees, took away my fight .. the smile that I had once worn, was no longer drawn on my face in a genuine fashion, and at this point, it felt like I just might .... Give up, throw in the towel, give them exactly what they'd been begging for, let my strength become weakness, because I just couldn't take another day of this anymore ...and I was seconds away from letting it all go ... and allowing myself to drift into a place where the darkness would take over, because at least in THAT SPACE ... I didn't have to worry about seeing the pain that was waiting to slap me in my face .. and it was all that I had left to give and STILL .. they each drank of my cup and never attempted to give me One, single, muthafuckin refill ...

So, when you tell the world about the chapter in YOUR book of OUR love ... ya know, after you've given them your side of the story and how you felt like I had given up on you ... Well, I just hope that you don't forget to mention the part about me loving you .. loving you more than you ever deserved, more than you ever expected, and even more than the times that you neglected to love me back ... because I was never keeping tabs until you gave me a reason to fire back

(Singing) Don't beat me like a drum, don't strum my pain with your fingers, don't pluck the strings on my guitar, unless your songs will heal my heart

SHOTS FIRED!

We live our entire lives hoping to find that someone who makes us feel complete ... that one we can love unconditionally, endlessly, completely,

with no regrets, no second thoughts…… and even when all the signs are clear and everything feels imperfectly perfect, we choose to question if what we're feeling is true.

It's in that moment where the insecurities, brokenness, pain and hurt from the past is revealed in the most transparent fashions ever. How do you love someone when the person you love is so broken that they're uncertainty flips like the fingers turning pages on your favorite book? I told myself a time or two, just remain patient in their moments of doubt and learn from the lessons being taught during the unsure phases of the Love Story you're creating.

AFTER ALL, IF U give up on the Love of your life, your life will never be full of the Love you deserve…. Right????

… BUT THERE IS A TWIST HERE…… FLOWERS CAN'T BLOOM WITHOUT, WATER, LIGHT, AND LOVE….. REMEMBER RELATIONSHIPS WORK THE SAME WAY. IF YOU AREN'T BLOOMING YOU ARE DYING. DON'T KILL YOURSELF … SOMETIMES THE HELP THEY NEED IS BEYOND YOUR CONTROL. It's okay to save your own life too, don't be fooled into believing that you don't matter …

BECAUSE YOU ABSOLUTELY DO!

PART 3

"FREE YOUR MIND"

💜 FREE YOUR MIND 💜

(REMINDERS AND MENTAL RELEASES DURING TOUGH MOMENTS)

💜 (Accountability and understanding)
People always see pretty bows and glitter until they are forced to face themselves in that very same mirror they've been using to fake the funk every day of their lives and the shame finally sets in ...

Now they find themselves standing there with a handful of stones, throwing them at the reflection that has been revealed, too afraid to face the truth ...

In their minds, it's easier to break the mirror!!

BREAKING THE MIRROR WON'T CHANGE THE TRUTH!

💜 (Living in a country that doesn't love you)
They say they ain't racist, they just hate us ... and every action, word, press conference, and law, tells us exactly how they feel ... like c'mon man pay attention, this shit can't be real ... They say we a threat to society, criminals and monsters, but we been forced to accept this same type of bullshit ass treatment all these years and they want us to be proud of our freedom. It's preposterous!!

They get to tuck their kids in bed at night, while good ole cousin jimmy prepares for his next nigga hunting joy ride .... in our neighborhoods .... playing target practice with our sons ...
It only takes a blind second to recognize that shit ain't right ...They shootin' guns for fun ... it's no wonder Lil buddy ain't even try to run, he

thought it was playtime with his toy gun, but boy was he wrong!! That baby neva made it home ... his family prepping psalms and songs to send to the funeral home, that baby gone!!

This shit is ridiculous ... U muthafuckas is some hypocrites ... we mess around and take our last breath, waiting on you to use your first to protect US... stop fuckin frontin ... And start by using ya corny ass privilege and stolen power to fuckin help us!! #DOSOMETHING

♥ (Sis Do Better)
Man, it's crazy to me that there are women in this world who pride themselves on seeing other women fail.... They do all they can to take good away from those who earned it and earned it honestly well...

Gives a whole new meaning to the phrase "Misery Loves Company"

Shit... All the Petty, Drama-filled BS and mess in your life, you oughtta be tired ... cause truth be told, you's a "Bitter Bitch"!! Emotionally, I'm tired and sick of the spill.... I'm getting to a point where I'm no longer buying the shit you sell!!! Don't want none of your 2-cent opinions, or your 99-cent advice, so don't try to feed me your surprise pies. I'm already nauseated and doubling over in pain, because I failed to say my grace before I filled my stomach with the lies you fed me on that fake ass China plate!!!....... #DAMN

♥SELF REFLECTION♥

As I slip into the world that no one else can see but me... I see myself crying, begging, and pleading with my reality to not let this be. I search for some type of clarification to hold the edges of my pages together as I try my best to match the ripped CORNERS of my soul with the broken crumbs of life that lay scattered on the floor of my heart's home inside my hollow chest.

"This house just isn't a home anymore", are the whispers that I hear as I struggle to regain consciousness, but nothing that I do is working and it's becoming clear that this is no longer my life.

Everything that I thought I had found in myself begins to diminish into the clouds that are no longer considered my cloud nine....no longer a natural high, but rather an escape to the only thing I can see clearly in front of me, because it's the only thing that resembles the me that I now see.

Blurry, sometimes high, and sometimes low.... barely recognizable in moments almost touching the ground ... but higher than the tires that burn rubber on the pavement of the road that I have chosen to travel. Love is complicated sometimes, but never perfect to touch, breathe, or see. It is an emotional roller-coaster rather it is spoken about in good or bad terms....it is a bundle of many adjectives, verbs, and nouns rolled into one moment ... Love is Life and Life is definitely worth living, but still, it seems impossible for many of us to continue to give it freely.... I'm taking the time now to simply, SEE ME!

PART 4

LOVE

(PEACE AND LIGHT)

 LOVE ♥

♥ <u>**LOVE**</u> ... *It DOESN'T COME WITH WARNINGS OR SIGNS that tell u when to be pretty, ready, or available.... it's untimely, unannounced, and spontaneous, it kind of does what it wants.*

It's magical
It's necessary
It's everything

Some may claim to not require love to survive ... I call them liars and I simply spread more love, because that's exactly what I need to get through this life.

♥ A SISTER'S LOVE ♥

A dedication to my Brother

We've lived our lives together for almost 40 years now...

but nothing could ever prepare me for this moment.

No way
No How

I've loved you since before I knew what love even was... Before we allowed our innocent years to disappear with the wind; before we could express a reason or cause!!

You comforted me in many of my moments of pain and sorrow and today all I want is to have another chance to hold you until tomorrow!!! I've tried my best to be strong for MOM, although I'm not certain how well I've done.

I've done my best to cherish your memories and your beautiful smile, so dear...but it's difficult for me to fight back the tears when you've been my best friend for so many years!!

I'm gonna miss our late-night convos and all the laughs and jokes we shared... No matter what we went through, you always re-assured me that you cared. I'm most definitely going to miss your cooking; Chef Wally didn't play in that kitchen...we ate good every day cause you was always hookin up something'.... Always putting those meals together, you coulda made it big preparing and selling your skills... you put some of the oddest combinations together and they still somehow tasted like Gourmet meals.

I'm not even certain that I can put together how I'm feeling right now.... "lost, broken, hurt, or emotional" don't even begin to describe the hole that is left in my heart.. I just keep replaying 12/21/16 in my head and I'm still trying to understand how!!! I don't want to let you go.. It's painful to let you leave, but I know that I must accept the fact that you have now earned your beautiful wings.

So, I bid my farewells as the tears roll down my face, and I pray that you are dancing AND keeping that warm beautiful smile on your handsome face. Watch over us down here.

I need you now, more than ever before, Lil Bro. Come sit with me from time to time. I reckon that will somehow make it easier but who knows.

Fly high my brother, for the sky is no longer the limit, you have now gained access to the next level of living and now it's your turn to RELAX, CHILL & KICK IT!! SAY HELLO TO DADDY & AUNTIE FOR US. Let them know we really miss them; no lie. We'll hold it down, until we meet again and trust me, your Baby Boy will be fine!!

I love u my brother, my best friend, and my partner in crime ... I'll always be here whenever you wanna talk, YOU KNOW I GOT U, at the drop of a dime!!

Love you always Wally

♥ ... 4 a fraction of a moment it felt like love with you and I'm happy for that feeling. I just hope I have the strength, knowledge, and understanding to decipher the code when it's time to decide if "THE ONE" Is standing in my face when that time really comes. Will I really know if it's real and worth holding onto? Or will I be so used up and mixed up in the expressions of fake love, that I allow my blessing(s) to slip right through my tiny fingertips?

Will I be able to make the best decision for the future of my life?

WILL I STILL BE ABLE TO SURVIVE AS A FUNCTIONAL & HAPPY WIFE???

♥TELL ME IT'S REAL♥

As I sit and think, on top of this cloud created amid the sip that I take followed by a puff of that loud... My creative juices are sparked by the sounds of the music that flows from the speakers beating directly behind my ears... all I can think about is the fact that I'm sitting in a time and space where seconds are now replacing the years. All I ever wanted to do was be someone's everything.... all that they ever needed in life covered in tiny little moments where I felt like I was the most beautiful woman in the world, even if I wasn't.

THAT ONE DAMN SHO' MADE ME FEEL LIKE I WAS THE ONLY WOMAN IN HIS BEAUTIFUL WORLD.

When he touched me, I knew I had been touched by the hands of an Angel. Wings broken and battered, but he possessed gentleness in his fingertipped touch. He stroked my soul with life and beautiful hints of hope... I was high on this cloud, no joke. Feels like there could be a good chance for more. Looks like there could be a NEW OPENING TO THAT door. I'm praying I don't have to hurt no more; please God tell me I don't have to hurt no more!

This beautiful man is reaching out to me, and I see it in his eyes he might just be perfect for me. I can see through the tunnels that we both dug deep, and I see a connection of souls at the beginning of a NEW sea ... I want this

Maybe I'm just vulnerable to love. I want it so badly that I'd try once more to give him Good Love....but I hope this is real ... all this greatness I feel. I just hope this is real.

PLEASE TELL ME IT'S REAL!!!

♥ WINDOWS, GLASS, & SUNSHINE ♥

I could stare into your eyes all day while you hold me close, because in your eyes I see truth, strength, courage, and wisdom. In your eyes I see pain endured, but I also see healing. I see a soul living to be free... trapped inside this body that's so damn appealing to me!!! I watched you closely as you began to peel away the broken glass from my eyelids... shattered in a million pieces, once blocking my vision for an extended period of time

I fought to keep them open, attempting to recover from this brokenness, and there you were.... so eager and willing...you helped me ... soothing my wounds as they healed in a season of refreshing positivity... your attentiveness and your precision to help me heal is a blessing to be able to experience.

I can see the sunshine peeking through... Caught off guard for a moment, afraid to move forward, not sure if my vision was playing tricks on me and I absolutely didn't want to let go of what could be ...the truth in it all is, WHEN I SEE YOU - I SEE ME... AND I don't see anything else around me

WHEN THEY ASK ME WHY I'M SMILING, I HAVE NO ANSWERS FOR THEM EXCEPT ...

H. E. R.

... Spirits touch and the energy fighting to escape bursts into millions of tiny specks of rainbow-colored dust.... It fills the air with a beautiful Multicolored ray of Sunshine. Makes me happy to be alive, feels good to confess that you are mine!

 PEACE ♥

♥ *PEACE .. It can sometimes seem so far out of reach that we lose track of how to obtain and maintain it ... learning when to let things or people go, when it comes to protecting our peace, is never easy, but it's always necessary.*

♥ *... In a time and space where everything around us becomes silent and none of the struggles of this world around us make noise at all. Where the only thing between us is the breath that we breathe right in front of our lips before they meet together in a passionate kiss...when nothing matters to us at all besides the happiness and desire to be free to love unconditionally, with no hesitation.... it is in that moment that I wish to be....AND THIS IS THE ONLY MOMENT THAT SOOTHES ME AND CONTINUES TO KEEP ME SMILING HAPPILY.... THE one thing that keeps the butterflies fluttering in my stomach.... that feeling of truth & peace where I am free to just be me...and never once have to question IF you still love me.... #Peace*

♥ RECOVERY ♥

It was so unexpected, yet so extremely necessary. It was in a moment in my life, where love was no longer in existence ... you found a warm place to reside in the crevices of my damaged heart, which had shut down some time ago. You slowly chipped away at the pieces of stone that covered the soft inside of my soul and you held me tightly in your strong hands, until the blood that was no longer circulating began to pump through my veins again. Finally, there was new life and just when I was so certain that I would never be able to love again, you gave me new hope for a brand-new life. One that could not be defined by a price tag or expensive gift, but an unconditional, yet expensively enriched expression of emotions that were so tightly embedded into my spiritual being that there was absolutely nothing left to gain but growth.

And it was then, that I felt myself nervously inhale & slowly exhale, in an excitedly, yet relaxed pace......

IT WAS YOU!!! You restored me and guided me towards recovery!

 I LIED

When I said I wouldn't give a damn the moment I gave up on you...said I wouldn't shed another tear at the slightest thought of you ... promised myself I wouldn't reminisce about the beautiful moments we shared together day after day ... begged myself to stay away from you so I wouldn't long for your touch – I talked myself out of calling your phone and interrupting your healing space, pretending not to miss hearing your voice or seeing that beautiful smile on your face.

I'd almost convinced myself that I was done with you. It's obvious that I can't fuck with you because you're uncertain, unsure, questioning your feelings ... ain't really shit I can do... and your inconsistency has absolutely no room in my life, and you know that so hey, I'll play it cool...I mean, it's fucked up, but still, IT'S COOL!! Not your fault that you've never known what real love felt like, never been with someone of genuine nature to love you despite your past life... Not your fault you didn't know what you and I had when we had it, but at the end of the day, I can't beg or force you to see me. I MEAN REALLY SEE ME!!!

It's true. I tried to convince myself that I didn't give a damn about you anymore, but I lied....and I ain't even a liar... BUT I lied to myself about my feelings for you ... but caring for you doesn't mean that I need you... I care enough about you to continue to wish you the absolute best and hope that you're doing well. I care enough to be proud of you, even though my heart still hurts that we failed.

WE COULDA BEEN GOOD TOGETHER, BUT BEING OUR BEST SELVES REQUIRED SEPARATE PATHS FOR US TO FOLLOW!

♥LIGHT♥

♥**_LIGHT_** ... **When you've been trapped in the darkness for so long, it can make you feel like light has passed you up forever, like it doesn't exist ... Don't believe the lies. Where there is darkness, there is always light. Find IT!!**

♥ *... And when my eyes open, I see colors... Some faded, some bold, some as vibrant as the sun peeking through my soul.. I wonder what they represent. Of everything past, future, and present ... I wonder if I'll see them again ... I wonder what color you represent in my world ...*

For now, I'll wait patiently ... mental paintbrushes in hand as my vivid mind twirls...

 BINGO

In the beginning of my new beginning, there was you ... You had somehow found a way to tap into those sapiosexual membranes of my skeletal frame, and as you entered me slowly ... you took your time with me. Made me remember all of the times that all of the others just had no time for me ... and how they'd only experienced a tiny glimpse of just one side of me, because they had never properly taken the time to penetrate the insides of me ...

But you ...you carefully studied me. Paid close attention to how my top lip quivered when you'd kiss that tiny spot behind my right earlobe ... and how I'd suddenly lost my train of thought when you kissed the inside of my left thigh as I tried so hard not to explode. You recreated me... turned my scattered showers into thunderstorms and my waterfalls into tsunamis

With the snap of your fingers ...the words you spoke to me, so eloquently and inviting became commands ... Commands that I so willingly desired to surrender to because you had this magical way of reassuring my mental in ways that I can't even begin to explain because you're simply not that simple. You're everything ... Your electrifying strokes give me power, kinda something like a real-life superhero ... and I've been a superwoman all my life, but nothing compares to this. For the very first time I realize ... I no longer have to fight ...I can let go!!

So I surrender, laying my whole life on the line, nipples standing at attention, I am down for whatever. There's no war for US to fight here ... because we're too busy creating light ... hear? Kinda sorta like the shooting stars and sonic booms that fill our moonlit dark skies ... see, we creatin' fireworks in places where our melanated bodies and souls collide...
You saved me

saved me for very last ... with your promise to savor the sweet taste of me for the rest of your forever, see ... I ain't even gotta think about it twice ... NO ONE HAS EVA DONE IT BETTA!

And so tonight...

I receive you, allowing you to make the connections that had been missed and skipped ova so many times in the past causing a continuous lack in pleasure. I slid down that slippery slope; before I could even think about turning back out of fear of losing control (inhale, exhale, slow moan) looks like you found that buried treasure. Now that SugahBoxxx you dipped into, that's all yours, all yours 4Eva ... BINGO!

💜 AFTER THE STORM 💜

MY FACE WAS HURTING from being slapped by Life SO MANY TIMES. TODAY I'M WAVING MY WHITE FLAG!! #ISURRENDER ... Broken Pieces are becoming whole again, and I'm lost in the words that bring me peace, strength, and comfort! The rain fell on me like a beating, drenching my soul in heavy armor, attempting to protect me from this unpredictable world we live in ... I realized something that I never knew ... the rain that was falling on me before today wasn't really rain at all...it was my tears ... the same ones I had been crying for so many years. I'd forgotten what the rain felt like but TODAY, it was peaceful, protective, encouraging ... IT WAS EVERYTHING I NEEDED ...

The rain was falling on me and hitting my sensitive skin hard, but I couldn't feel any pain, because the pain had been washed away and replaced with love. That love had created a barrier of protection around me, which allowed me to experience pain in a different aspect. I collected the rain in a jar, pure clean and true ... and I saved it ... this water was made to be shared with you. I'll hold onto it until you decide to show up, to remind me of how beautiful life is when you learn to grow through your pain and fight for your life. I imagine we will enjoy this glass of rainwater together to quench our souls with the beverage that has been prepared for us, to help us on our journey forward as we enjoy a life together ... it's what we'll have left when everything else has passed away and ceases to exist in the world we live in. DANCE IN THE RAIN WITH ME AND LET YOUR SOUL BE NOURISHED!

drop everything now, and meet me in the rain

 TRY AGAIN

Yesterday I went to reach for you, but you weren't there to reach back. I imagined how beautiful it would feel to be stuck together again, like the straps on the back of our favorite snap backs ... I wanted to remember how it felt to be all up in your space ... You, kissing me where my skin becomes spirit, loving me, planting kisses on my face ... replacing the taste of my tears with the taste of your love on my plate ... but you've been gone for a while now ... and yet no one is worthy of taking your place

I'm not exactly sure why I'm still waiting ... we haven't been a thing for a while now ... maybe someday, I'll find a way to move on completely, when my mind can somehow forget how you made my heart smile ... like back when there wasn't a blemish in the love that we shared for each other ...

Man ... what a beautiful time

All those magical moments we created when the connections pulled us in through the portals of our eyes and our minds ... and we never asked why ... not one single time ... Because I was yours and you were most definitely mine.

We were every wish and dream that represented love, in the middle of our own beautiful disaster of happiness ... where the sun met the land and the trees met the wind, somehow, we bloomed ... but we forgot something ... we forgot to water the roots that grew beneath the grass ... and all those careless mistakes that we made caused our foundation to crash.

CAN'T YOU SEE ... we failed ourselves ... DAMN ... I miss you ... I think that it's time we do things differently this time around and perhaps, rebuild ourselves ... TOGETHER ... let me love you ... PROPERLY!!

I'm sure that we can get it right this time around, I'm thinking we should try this again ... let's see how strong we can love out loud, let's love each other until this lifetime ends and then start all over ...

I'm askin' ... Can we try again?

I think it's time that we water our gardens, so tell me .. are you still down?

(The aftermath)

 FOCUS

(Singing) Me ... Can you Focus on ... Me ... Baby can you focus ... On me

Let me taste you ... Take every inch of you inside of me, I want you to do things to me that you've only seen in your dreams

Until tonight

Take me ... Own every part of me in pleasure ... make me moan for it ... hell, I'd be more delighted if you make me beg for it baby ... and I promise to remind you of how every inch of this Pussy was absolutely, intentionally ... made for it ... FOCUS

On me

Let me watch you ... let me watch you deep dive inside these walls, paint the mirrors with erotic-induced steam ... place your head ... inside my cookie jar and don't you dare forget to lick the cream ...

FOCUS. ARE YOU STILL WITH ME?

Testing ... one ... two ....Taste Me. You know you want ... to ... warning, this is not a dream ... I want you on your knees ... Right here ... right now ... Now ... FOCUS .. ON ...

(Singing) ME ... Can you Focus on ... Me ... Baby can you focus ... on me ..FOCUS!

♥ PROMISES I'M GLAD I MADE TO MYSELF

I made a promise to myself one day... that I would never give up on me again... not only because I had 2 beautiful young boys at the time that were staring me in my eyes each day, as I suffered with a very difficult battle of depression...BUT when that 2 became 3, the struggle which was already significant now became VERY REAL!! Nothing about the choices I had to make for the sake of those babies was easy... I cried many nights, searching for a reason not to blame myself for all of the turmoil that was currently spilling over in my life, while still trying to hold on to the strength I had left

... I just needed a little bit of something to keep going, that's what I told myself each day... DEEP DOWN INSIDE, I just wasn't certain I could get through that storm!!

NOW HERE I AM YEARS LATER, proud of the growth and the strength I've built up inside to keep moving forward!!! Nothing on this earth can take that away from me and I'm so grateful....to just have enough love inside of me to continue this journey of life, with no regrets, no grudges, and no hatred.

After all of that pain, I walk away today with valuable lessons learned and new friends who helped me get to my happy place.... and that is something so beautiful it can't be described or put into words that can do it any justice.

Life definitely finds creative ways to knock us down and test our strength to get back up and fight again!!! THAT BITCH OUGHTA BE T'IIIIEED OF FOOLIN WITH ME BY NOW ... but if she ever comes back for another round, this time, I'll be ready... LET'S BATTLE BITCH!!!

PEACE Love & LIGHT

To those responsible for the emotions and expressions in this book.

I thank you! Although there were moments where I felt like I was too broken to move on, each of you who played an active role in my journey, no matter how our paths crossed or where the journey with us may have ended. At the end of the day, lessons were learned and without the moments of experience that were shared, I would not be the survivor I am today! I take away the love, the pain, the hurt, the laughter, and I leave it all in the pages of my books, poems, songs, and life notes. Thank you all for giving me something to write about. Thank you for forcing me to keep the promises that I made to myself and allowing Karma to do its job, as I continue to do mine!

Dedications & Appreciations

I dedicate this, my first (many more to come) book of poetry and life notes first, to my family and close friends. Thank you for your never-ending support and motivation. Thank you for believing in me, even in moments where I didn't believe in myself. Thank you for pushing me to always be my best self, by challenging me to do things that I did not push myself to do out of fear. You are the reason that this book has come to fruition. You believed in me since I was a small child, and nothing could have prepared me for this next step in my journey better than the love that you have poured into me over the years of my life. I pray that this book makes you proud and provides you with many smiles along the way, knowing that you have birthed and created a solid foundation that can never be broken.

To my 3 piece, My Gremlins, My 3 Young Kings, My handsome boys,

You are more important to me than you will ever know or understand. You saw me and loved me in my most vulnerable and raw moments and you helped push me through some of the most painful times of my life. You gave my life meaning and purpose, before I ever knew I had a meaningful purpose here on earth. Thank you for loving me through every phase of my life and still trusting me to care for you on my darkest nights. Everything I do, I do for you. I love you more than words can ever express. Thank you for your never-ending support! I love you forever!
I LOVE YOU ALL!!

Secondly, I want to dedicate this project to all the strangers I have met over the last 15 years who have become family. Thank you for the inspiration you have given me to chase my dreams. I wish I had the page space to name all of you, but that would mean writing books and books dedicated to expressing my gratitude. Please know, you are more than a

name, number, or face to me. You represent the burning flame that continues to shine bright inside the walls that protect my beating heart. You are the reason I continue to live life to the fullest with no regrets. Your light has given me the strength I needed over the years, enabling me to grow in love and light and for that, I am forever grateful! Thank you.

Lastly, I dedicate this book to my late Brother Walter Roy Hunter, III, and Aunt Gwindale Boson! Although you are not here to witness this in the flesh, I know that you are watching over me in spirit and that you are cheering me on, smiling hard, and laughing loud. Although it pains me to not be able to share this with you in the flesh, I want to thank you for all your love and support while you both were here on this earth. You two loved me unconditionally and without any regrets. Our family is not the same without you two in it, but we will continue this journey and I will not let you down.

Rest on, my loves! Fly high my beautiful doves!

To My Supporters and Readers:

It is my hope that my expression of words finds you in a place and time where you need it the most or that you know someone who does. May the heart of each person who reads or hears the words shared in this book be comforted, protected, and repaired, and may your soul be healed as you continue on your life journey

#PeaceLoveAndLight. Journey well! Let's Ride!

ABOUT THE AUTHOR

Krystal "LyriK Hunter" Dorsey, born in Midland, TX, a current resident of Dallas, Tx, where she has lived, since her early teens, is a proud mother of three young men, and has enjoyed writing since her early grade school years.

LyriK is a vibrant, professional performing artist who has been blessed to stand before audiences all over the country. Showing her skills in places like Texas, California, Georgia, Tennessee, North Carolina and many others, she giftedly weaves her life lessons and wisdom into her poetry for the purpose of teaching others. She participates in community shows and events for The Dallas Museum of Arts (Arttitude_DFW), F.L.O.W. (Masterpiece Ent, Dallas, TX), Pan African Connection (2 Inspire Peace Inc/AIH, Dallas, TX), and many others. Leading the way as CEO/Owner of "The Brown Sugah Lounge", LyriK (and her Team) make up this powerfully poetic Dallas-based group that provides a safe space to release and heal through spoken word and poetic expressions. LyriK's personal goal is to help society heal one poem at a time.

Inside this personal collection of poetic writings and journey notes, are some of the most intimate, traumatizing, and beautiful moments of LyriK's life, and how she managed to find the light in the darkest places. This book WILL save souls, heal hearts, and change lives ...

SPONSORSHIP/DONATION ACKNOWLEDGEMENTS

Thank you to my sponsors and launch team who donated their time, love, encouragement, and finances to help see this book through to its physical form. Because of each of you, I have been able to vulnerably, yet freely give of myself in more ways than one.

Your endless support does not go unnoticed!

Please support these businesses and others in our community who continue to give of themselves and their talent daily. It's one thing to say you support and it's another to actually do it. Our community deserves to have people in it who care enough about the success of those around them, to lend their services and time in an effort to grow and build together. We are only as great as those around us. Help us build a greater world by supporting those who make it their duty to support others.

BUSINESS SPONSORS

The Brown Sugah Lounge Family
(Reign, Alchemy, Gno, Alex, Keith, Metcher)
Please Follow on all social media platforms:
IG: @thebrownsugahloungellc
FB: @thebrownsugahlounge
TikTok: @thebrownsugahoungedfw
Twitter & Snapchat coming soon

Email for Booking: thebrownsugahlounge@gmail.com or send a message on the website at: www.thebrownsugahlounge.com

Sheer Alternatives.com

Sheer Alternatives would like to esteem Krystal Dorsey aka Lyrik Hunter highly for this accomplishment and the courage shown in sharing her personal growth and life experiences with us all. We salute you and pray you continue to be the light for the world around you to see. Peace

2 INSPIRE PEACE INC.(AIH Collective)
Please Follow on all social media platforms:
IG: @2inspirepeaceinc
FB: @2InspirePeaceInc
WEBSITE: https://www.2inspirepeace.org/

"... love you for no reason at all, you are more than deserving of celebration ... You're major Sis #TakeUpSpaceSis"

PERSONAL SPONSORS

My Immediate Family
(Mommy-Sherrie, Pops-Wilson, Sons-Cager, IV, Cardale, Davonte, Cousins-Ashley, Darius, Cory, Heaven, Cory, Jr., Harmony, Children's father-Cager, III – Thank you for giving of yourselves, your time, your money, and your support)

Kimberly Wilson
*Yolande Dillard **(Owner of Esinedy Creations)***
Rissa Dawn
Aletha Hines
Charles Kelly
Erica Grady
Melanie Johnson
Erica Johnson
*Imauriah Chanel **(Owner of LocdByMauri)***
*Brittany Lewis **(Owner of A Hundred XOXO)***
Te Mathis
Brandi Lewis
Tamara Palmer
Brennon Lamar
Kent Helvey
*Angel Chavis**(Owner of Customz by Angel)***
Tricia Christian
Roshun Chisolm

LAUNCH TEAM

The Brown Sugah Lounge
(Reign, Alchemy, Gno, Alex, Keith, Metcher)
Kimberly Wilson
Erica Grady
Sharia Todd
Nikisha Patton Handy
Crystal Thomas
Reem Mughrabi
Dorothy Williams
Sherrie Hunter
Kaneesha Jackson
Ashley Rhodes
Erica Johnson
Sharyl Deamer
Demetrice Buford
Cager Dorsey
Cardale Dorsey
Davonte Jackson
Diandra Wade

LOVE & LIFE THRU THE EYEZ OF LYRIK

www.ingramcontent.com/pod-product-compliance
Lightning Source LLC
Chambersburg PA
CBHW070550090426
42735CB00013B/3138